Gran's New Blue Shoes

Written by Roderick Hunt

Illustrated by Nick Schon,
based on the original characters
created by Alex Brychta

OXFORD
UNIVERSITY PRESS

Read these words

n**ew**	dr**ew**
ph**ew**	tr**ue**
kn**ew**	gl**ue**
fl**ew**	bl**ue**

BLUE SHOE GLUE

Mum had some good news.
"Gran is going to meet the Queen,"
she said.

A car drew up. It was Gran.

"I am going to meet the Queen,"
she said.

"Good for you," said Mum.
"What great news."

"I will need to choose a new dress … and a hat … and new shoes," said Gran.

Gran got a new dress. She had a
new hat and new blue shoes.

The time flew by. At last, Mum
took Gran to London. Biff, Chip and
Kipper went too.

"The Queen lives here," said Gran.

Oh no! The heel on Gran's new, blue shoe came off.

Gran was upset.

"I can't meet the Queen with no heel on my shoe," she said.

"I can lend you some blue boots,"
said a lady.

"I can glue the heel on," said a
man. "I have a tube of glue in
my van."

A big car drew up. A flag flew
on the roof.

Chip ran up to the car.

"Stop that boy," called a man.

"Excuse me. Will you help us?"
called Chip.

The car stopped and a man
got out.

It was the Duke.

"The heel has come off Gran's new blue shoe," said Chip.

"I'll see what I can do," said the
Duke. "Wait by this gate."

Later, a man came to the gate. He
had a box. It was full of blue shoes.

"You can choose from these shoes,"
he said.

Gran went to meet the Queen.

"I do like your shoes," said
the Queen.

"Gran's blue shoes will be big
news," said Biff.

Talk about the story

What happened to Gran's new pair of blue shoes?

What was wrong with the blue boots?

How did the Duke help Gran?

What would you wear if you went to meet the Queen?

Rhyming words

Read each word on the blue shoe box.
Find a rhyming word on the red shoe box.

shoes   boot
blue   moon

flute   blew
prune   news